Minecraft: AWESOME Building Ideas for You

By
Minecraft books

Table of Contents

Introduction

Building is a great part of Minecraft. Its part of what let's your creativity flow, you can build what you want, you can make yourself the biggest house or castle. You can work on making many different types of buildings and structures. Your imagination is the limit.

Of course it's always nice to pick up some new tips and tricks, to see how others have build their houses, how they decorated them and how you can do all that too. So read on and find out everything you need to know.

A Fountain

Mix this up with your new garden and your house will begin to look extremely fancy.

A Fireplace

A fireplace is great way to change up the usual dull room. Adding lava is optional but can be a great feature.

Interior Decorating

Building the skeleton of a house and adding different features will only bring you halfway. You still need to decorate it and make your house more than just empty rooms.

Furniture

Let's start with furniture. They're a couple of different way to make furniture look somewhat realistic in Minecraft.

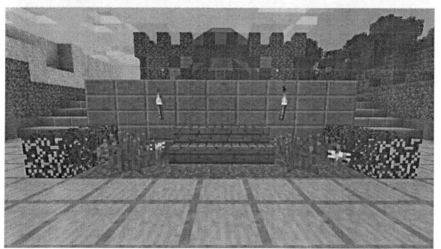

Tables

The simplest way to build a table is to place a single piece of fence and place a pressure plate on top of it.

Chairs

To create a chair, place down a half block and place signs on 3 of the 4 sides to create a simple armchair.

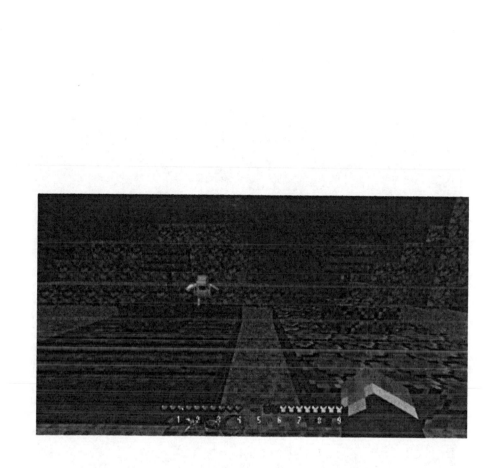

Counters

Use normal blocks in the right areas to create a counters look.

Desks

Add a few tables together and place chairs at them to create a simple desk look.

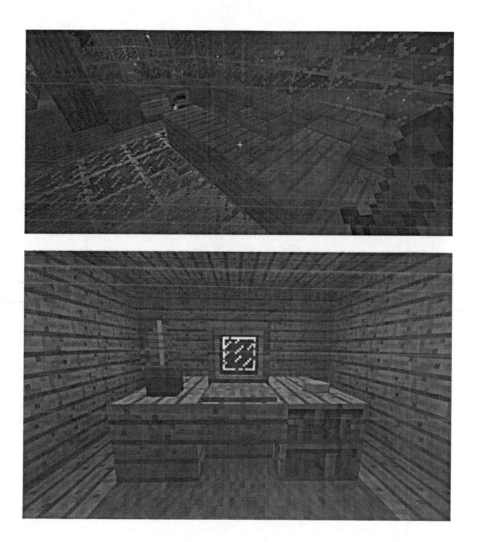

Paintings

A Massive Variety

There is a massive variety of different Minecraft paintings they range from a single block to massive several block masterpieces. Keep destroying and replacing your paintings until you find one that you like.

Picking the Right Spot

Picking the right spot can be a little tricky and might take some planning ahead. Finding the perfect painting for the perfect spot is a perfect addition to any home.

House Building

Building a home of some kind is something that practically everyone has done in Minecraft. You need one just to survive the first night. But then days and days of in game time go by and you've built up your house up but you just don't know how to build it up from there. The first thing you need to decide is the style of your Minecraft house.

Blueprints

Wood Home

Step One:

Dig an 8x10 hole in the ground and fill it with a single layer of oak wood planks.

Step Two:

Cover the edge of the wood square with oak wood (or spruce wood if you want a variety) one block high. Leave a two block wide gap in the middle of the wall for the door.

Step Three:

Add in 2 blocks of glass in all the areas in the screenshot above to create windows. Fill in the rest of the edge with more oak wood. Make sure you put some blocks on top of the doors as well.

Step Four:

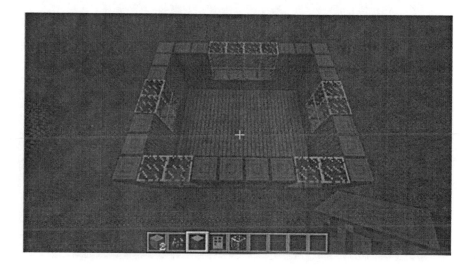

Build a full layer of spruce wood planks on top of that to create a roof. Make sure you add an extra one block over hang along the edge of the roof.

Step Five:

Finally fill in a single layer of spruce wood planks one block smaller than the previous layer. You've just completed your wood home!

Brick House

Step One:

Dig an 8x6 hole in the ground and fill it with a single layer of oak wood planks (or any type of planks if you'd like to change it up).

Step Two:

Cover the outside edge with a single layer of bricks one block tall. Remember to leave a single block empty for the door.

Step Three:

Add glass for windows a single block tall in the spots in the above screen shot. Fill the remaining border with more bricks.

Step Four:

Cover the entire area with bricks. Make sure that the entire area is filled in.

Step Five:

Cover the top layer with oak wood planks and build out one layer of oak wood stairs to create a nice sloping effect.

Step Six:

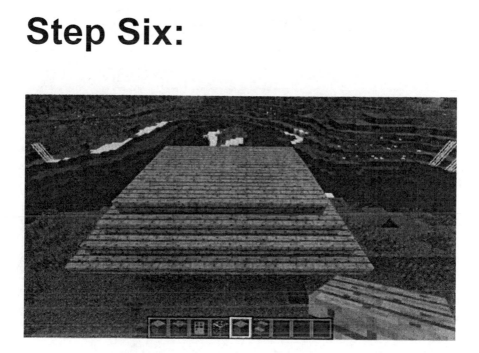

Do the same thing with the next layer just be sure to move the layer one block in on all sides.

Fortress Tower

Step One:

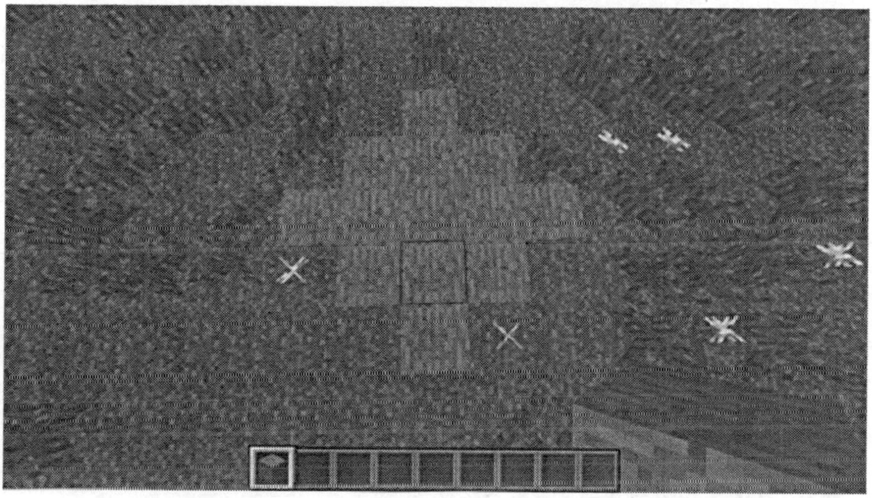

Dig a 3x3 hole in the ground and fill it with stone (or cobblestone). Now dig a hole outside of the hole, one for each side and fill it with stone too.

Step Two:

Now build up two blocks around the edge of the base. Leave an empty space for the door.

Step Three:

Build another layer of stone on top of everything including on top of the door. Now put a block of glass on each outside section and fill the rest of the layer in with glass.

Step Four:

Build three more layers of stone on top and then add another layer of glass and stone on top of that. Repeat that set up of 3 layers of stone and one of glass 3 more times.

Step Five:

Build an entire layer of stone on top of the last layer of glass. Leave a single hole for the ladder. Build out the stone one block further to create an overhang.

Step Six:

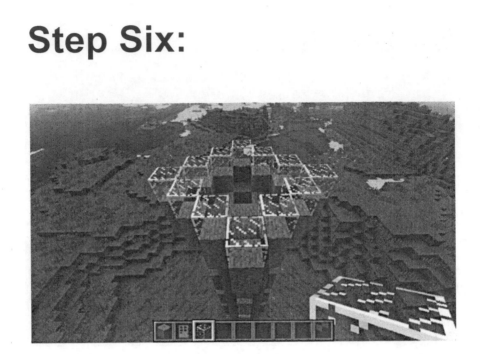

On the edge only, build one layer of stone and one layer of glass.

Step Seven:

Fill in the entire layer with stone.

Step Eight:

Now build two more layers, each layer one short of the edge until you only need to place a single block on top!

Step Nine:

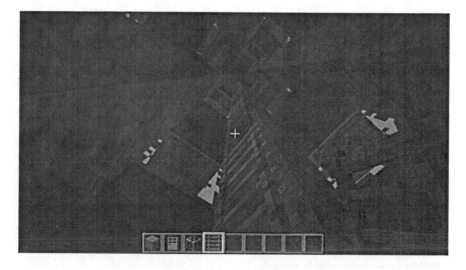

Now go inside and start building a ladder on the block opposite of the door on the right all the way to the top of your tower. Now go up top and enjoy the view!

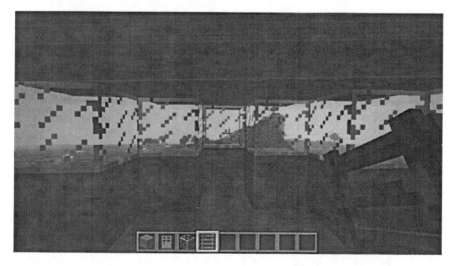

Tree House

Step One

Find a nice tree in the jungle biome, preferably the tallest one.

Step Two

Clear off the top of the tree, make it as flat as possible.

Step Three

Create a layer of wood planks; leave a little section in the middle for the bottom floor. How big is going be depends on the size of your tree.

Step Four

Clean up the tree a little by digging down through the center. Only go down about three or four blocks.

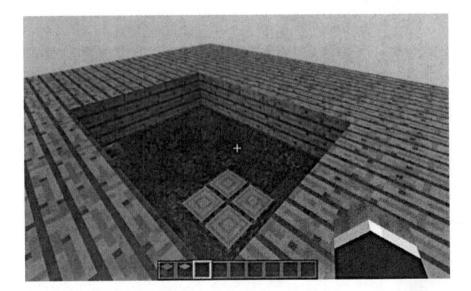

Step Five

Build up some planks around the outside edges of your new basement level below your main floor, create both a floor and the walls but leave one side open for the balcony.

Step Six

From the side of your balcony that's open build out a balcony for about 4 to 5 blocks.

Step Seven

Use fences around the edge of your balcony to create a nice railing.

Step Eight

On the inside of your basement carve out a little section of the wall and place some glass to create a window.

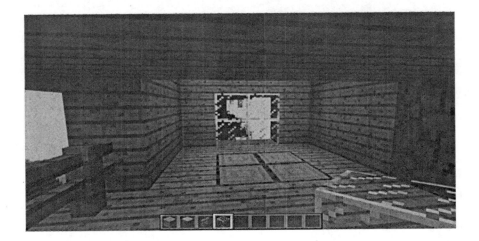

Step Nine

On the top for build out wood blocks and glass 2 blocks high to create the walls and the windows.

Step Ten

Now build out the entire roof of your building with wood planks, I left a little section of glass to create a sunroof.

Step Eleven

On the bottom of your basement, destroy one block and replace it with a ladder so you can easily get to your tower using both the vines and your ladder.

Step Twelve

Play some more ladders going from your basement to main floor. Now your beautiful tree house is completely finished!

Small Outpost

Step One

Create a two by two hole in the ground.

Step Two

Surround the hole with glass; leave a single opening for the door.

Step Three

Place wood planks or stone on top of the glass.

Step Four

Now create a roof for your little outpost with wood planks or stone.

Step Five

Add a door to your outpost.

Step Six

Add both a crafting table and a furnace on the inside.

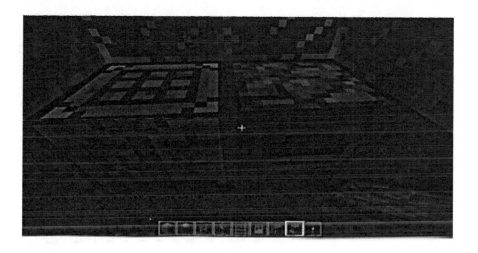

Step Seven

Place some torches on the inside to shed some light on your new outpost.

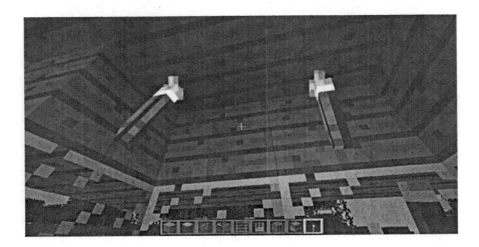

Step Eight

Finally build some torches around the outside of your outpost to keep any monsters at bay during the night.

Hidden Stone Fortress

Step One

Pick a nice spot made of stone on the mountainside.

Step Two

Clear any dirt from the entrance to make it as flat as possible.

Step Three

Dig out an area about 5 by 5. You can make yours bigger or smaller depending on how big you want your fortress to be.

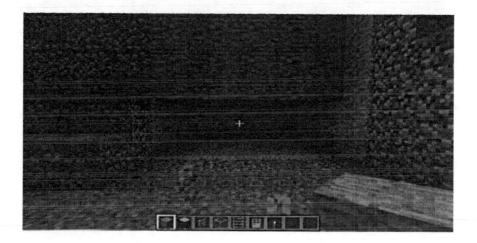

Step Four

Build a wall at the entrance of your fortress, leaving only a small space for a door.

Step Five

Add in any door you want, I've chosen to use an iron door, as it's the most safe.

Step Six

Make sure your entire fortresses well lit, place torches whenever you can.

Step Seven

Dig down one more layer, and add a staircase to your door and a button to your iron door, if you have one.

Step Nine

To the left, build out into the wall and make a 2 by 2 hallway to a room that's 4 by 4. Make sure to add as many torches as you need.

Step Ten

Place down three large chests, this'll be the treasure and storage room.

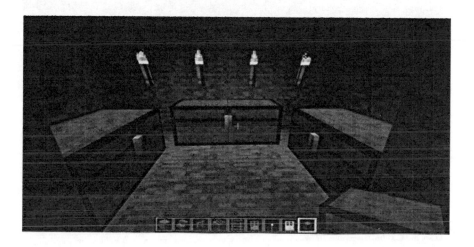

Step Eleven

Repeat step nine on the other side.

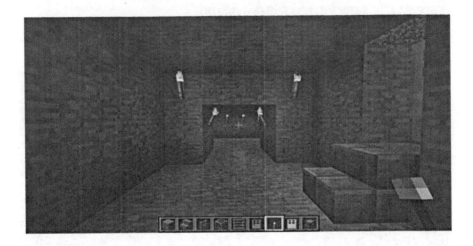

Step Twelve

Fill this room with furnaces, crafting tables, cauldrons, and brewing stands. This is the crafting and creation room.

Step Thirteen

In the main hall dig a 5 x 5 area across from the stairs. Make sure it's also three blocks tall.

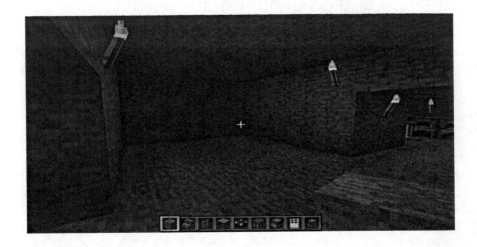

Step Fourteen

Cover the walls with bookshelves and place an enchantment table right in the center.

Step Fifteen

In the middle of your main room dig a hole four blocks deep.

Step Sixteen

At the bottom of hole create a room that's 5 by 5. This will be the bedroom.

Step Seventeen

You can decorate the entire room with paintings, and place a bed down in the main area. Be sure to place a lot of torches as well.

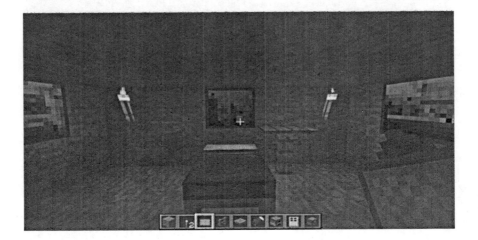

Step Eighteen

Build a ladder going up hole. And now your entire stone fortress is completed!

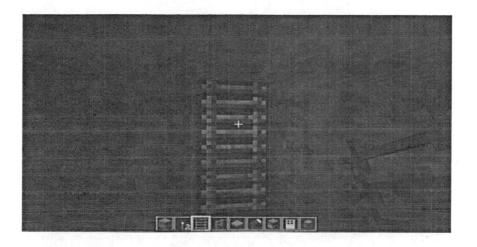

Style

Traditional

This is the basic style of any Minecraft house. It's made entirely of wood, stone, dirt, and glass. It's the most basic and simplest style you can build in.

Sleek

This style of Minecraft home is usually made out of entirely glass and other smooth blocks liked smelted stone or gold for the richer players.

Unique

This style is very different from the usual homes of Minecraft. They usually look nothing like homes at all and instead like other objects such as a pirate ship or balloon.

Of course there are many other styles out there but these three styles should give you some idea of what kind of house you want to build.

Building Your Home

The key to every great Minecraft house is to plan it from the foundation up. Start by flattening out your foundation and lay the first level. Place down the floor of the first level and use it to plan out how large you want your entrance and other rooms to be here. It's best to plan your layout out ahead of time or you don't need to constantly be rebuilding.

Next up are the walls and windows. Start building up your walls to the height you want them at. Be sure to plan out your windows and doors ahead of time.

Once you've built your first floor you should add a ceiling. Continue adding floors in this manner until you have as many levels as you want. Just remember to add stairs or a ladder so you can easily reach each floor.

Adding on a roof is usually the simplest step. Most Minecraft houses won't require anything more than the basic flat roof. Just don't let that hold your creativity back. You can easily add a glass roof or create a small roof top balcony.

Materials

Picking which materials you want to build your building with has a lot to do with what style of building you're building. Each different block goes well with a certain style.

Cobblestone

Cobblestone is a basic and cheap way to build your home. It looks alright but definitely isn't an eye pleaser. Smelting cobblestone into stone is a quick and easy way to quickly make your house look much nicer.

Wood

Wood is a great material to build your home out of. You can use the raw wood for more of a cabin look or craft it down into planks if you like a more natural looking house.

Dirt

Perfect for building a house that blend into the countryside. It doesn't look as good if you're building is above ground.

Brick

Brick is a much more expensive block to build. It really adds an authentic feel to practically any house. It can even make a cave seem like a cozy home.

Pick the material that you think is going to suit your house the best, and don't be afraid to experiment and let your imagination run wild. You can try building with all kinds of blocks from wool to diamond.

Add-ons

Adding new elements to your home will make it stand out that much more, it will be more unique and become a nicer place to spend your time in game. So think about adding any of the following to your home.

A Balcony

A simple balcony can add a nice touch while a grand balcony can be the highlight of your home.

A Garden

Spice up the area around your house, add a variety of flowers or just create a nice row of trees leading up to your house. Make small garden or a large one, do whatever fits your home.

A Tower

Often considered a castle only feature, a tower can be a great land mark for quickly finding your house in the future, not to mention it can make your house that much more imposing.

Crafting and Enchanting

The Most Important Room in the House

The crafting and alchemy rooms are some of the most important rooms of the house; they are where all the action takes place. Many people even build their storerooms right next to them for easy access. Building the perfect set up is very important.

Crafting

The basics are usually all that's required. The main area will need a crafting table, a brewing stand, and a furnace. It's usually a good idea to have a chest or two near by so you can quickly and easily store and retrieve everything you need while crafting.

Enchantment

It's important to have as many bookshelves around your enchantment table as possible. That way you maximize the level of power from the enhancements. It's usually a good idea to fill up a small room with bookshelves while keeping a small space in the middle for the table.

Conclusion

Your imagination is the limit while you build your house. Never stop innovating and trying out different combinations and new things.

Bonus Section

Thank you for reading this book. I hope you enjoyed it. Gaming is very near and dear to my heart and I enjoy every moment I spend playing my favourite games.

If you liked this book, and are interested in more, I invite you to join my "Customer Only" newsletter at http://awesomeguides.net/. I publish all my best stuff there for free, only for my customers.

If you're a Minecraft fan like I am, I'm sure you'll like my other best-selling releases:

1. Minecraft: Awesome Building Ideas for You
2. Amazing Minecraft Secrets You Never Knew About
3. Minecraft All-In-One Quick Guide! Master your Minecraft skills in Everything!

In my strategy guides, I share neat tips and tricks to help you get better at gaming. From Candy Crush to Dragonvale, you'll find strategy guides for a wide variety of addictive games.

2. <u>Dragonvale: The Complete Guide:
   Amazing Cheats, Gems, Breeding and
   MORE!</u>
3. <u>Candy Crush Saga Best Tips, Tricks
   and Cheats!</u>

We also have an awesome Minecraft course
on Udemy – an instructor led online learning
platform.

   1. <u>All about Minecraft: A complete
      educational course</u>

Have fun gaming!
Egor

CPSIA information can be obtained at www.ICGtesting.com
Printed in the USA
LVOW10s0905250614

391642LV00002B/174/P